MW01114115

COOKIES
BAKE SALE
SUGAR
FLOUR

1ST
ANNUAL

COLOR
TEST
PAGE
I ♥ U

I ♥ U

OPCORN
POP

$3
LOCAL
HONEY

YOU'RE SO CUTE! ♥

OATS

Printed in the USA
CPSIA information can be obtained
at www.ICGtesting.com
LVHW071133121124
796389LV00018B/307
* 9 7 8 2 6 4 0 2 2 0 6 0 4 *